This book is for _____

Today's date is:_____

One year review date: _____

Three year review date:_____

Five year review date:_____

## Why this book/planner?

This book contains various ways for MEN to identify goals, plan, express themselves, learn new things and keep records. Planning refers to the process of deciding *what* to do and *how* to do it. I want to provide healthy ways to assist MEN in summarizing key principles and practices in order to have effective planning, particularly in their personal life and daily living. Most of all, I want to end the stigma associated with "feelings" and break society's norms of what a MAN is, or isn't, supposed to be. The benefits of effective planning take into account many diverse perspectives and impacts. The education that can be obtained in this planner can assist MEN for generations to come! Planning will help in your life by assisting in the decision-making process in order to identify and implement the most effective ways to achieve goals, no matter how minor or grand. Do you find that there is never enough time for everything? If so, it is probably because you are not scheduling your time effectively. This is important for your personal *and* professional life. There are fundamental definitions written in a way for all young MEN and adults to understand. While many people think of productivity as it relates to their job, you also want to be productive at home. Stress has many forms as well, but a common denominator is the feeling of being *overwhelmed*. As you might imagine, planners can help you stay healthy in a wide range of ways.

Another benefit of using a planner is, since you are sticking to a schedule for all of the *mandatory* responsibilities, it will create free time for your own artistic endeavors, whether that means working on a hobby or trying something new.

This book will also be a way to educate, or enlighten, MEN on the advantages of things like affirmations, expressing themselves, values, goals, MENtal HEALth awareness, etc.

2

Lastly, another good way to use this journal is for keeping track of changes, whether an increase or decrease that occurs in your day-to-day life. You, or the people around you, can monitor your progress.

In this guide, boys and MEN will be able to write or draw, learn a few definitions, plan for the future, and keep notes, among other things.

I will be giving my personal spin on the key words and phrases used in order to help move things along. I would rather you understand what I am referencing opposed to a bunch of jargon that will have you questioning the usage of this guide.

Throughout this book, you will be asked to "Express it on the next pages..." Take that as your way to creatively write out or draw your answers.

Enjoy, and whatever you do, just express yourself!

# Contents

## *Goals*

When it comes to goals, break them down into two parts. You may be familiar with this, but separating **short-term goals** and **long-term goals** are easy ways to distinguish between them. A goal is an idea of a desired result that you envision, plan, and commit to achieve. This can be something you want to obtain in your business, relationship, family, school, or daily life.

For the sake of this guide, your short-term goals should be six months or less and your long-term goals should be one year and beyond.

**Instead of me sharing my list with you, the purpose of this is for you to be engaging, therefore:**

**What are your personal goals?**

**How can you better accomplish your goals?**

**Have you accomplished any goals in the last year?**

**Create 10-15 short-term goals.**

**Create 5-10 long-term goals.**

*Express it on the next pages...*

# *Write it out, MAN! - Short Term Goals*

_____

_____

_____

_____

_____

_____

_____

_____

_____

_____

_____

_____

_____

_____

_____

_____

_____

_____

_____

_____

_____

_____

_____

_____

# *Write it out, MAN! - Depression*

_____

_____

_____

_____

_____

_____

_____

_____

_____

_____

_____

_____

_____

_____

_____

_____

_____

_____

_____

_____

_____

_____

_____

_____

_____

_____

_____

_____

# Draw it out, MAN! - Depression

## AbandonMENt

In many of us, abandonMENt invites a type of anxiety that some people experience when faced with the idea of losing someone they care about. Everyone deals with death or the ending of relationships in their lifetime. Loss is a natural part of life. If not handled properly, this can also prevent the developMENt of other healthy bonds with new friends, partners, or relationships.

**Have you been abandoned?**

**Have you ever abandoned someone?**

**Have you cycled through relationships or engaged in numerous shallow relationships?**

**Have you mistakenly sabotaged a relationship?**

**Did you knowingly push away a partner so you won't feel hurt if they leave?**

**Do you cling to unhealthy relationships or stayed in relationships despite a desire to leave?**

**Do you need constant reassurance to demand emotional guarantees?**

*Express it on the next page...*

## Write it out, MAN! - AbondonMENt

_____

_____

_____

_____

_____

_____

_____

_____

_____

_____

_____

_____

_____

_____

_____

_____

_____

_____

_____

_____

_____

_____

_____

*Draw it out, MAN! - Grief*

## *Anger*

Anger is one of the basic huMAN emotions that can be related to the "Fight, Flight, or Freeze" response of our sympathetic nervous system. It involves a strong, uncomfortable, and hostile response to a perceived provocation, hurt or threat. This prepares huMANs to fight. Anger can have many physical and MENtal consequences.

Physical conditions, such as increased heart rate, elevated blood pressure, and increased levels of adrenaline and noradrenaline. Major feelings when met with anger are experienced and displayed behaviorally, cognitively, and physiologically.

**How do you control your anger?**

**Do you have any physical symptoms when angry (teeth clinching, palm sweeting, facial expressions)?**

**What do you do when you are angry?**

**How do you prevent being angry?**

**Opposed to being angry, what can you do?**

*Express it on the next page...*

## *Write it out, MAN! - Anger*

_____

_____

_____

_____

_____

_____

_____

_____

_____

_____

_____

_____

_____

_____

_____

_____

_____

_____

_____

_____

_____

_____

_____

_____

_____

_____

_____

# Draw it out, MAN! - Anger

## Substance Use

For as long as one can remember, substance use has been the go-to coping mechanism for MEN. From alcohol, marijuana, prescription pills, to harder substances like cocaine and heroin, many MEN have been identified as heavy users of various substances. The results of this alienation are dramatic: When MEN are not in relationships or do not have children, they are less likely to complete substance use treatMENt. Previous studies indicate that the majority of American MEN over 12 years of age (82.6%) had used alcohol at least once in their lifetime. The data indicates that 9% of MEN reported heavy alcohol use (five or more drinks at one time in the previous month), compared to 2% of woMEN. Approximately 34% of the sample reported using illicit drugs. Studies also indicate that drug use patterns vary significantly by racial and ethnic groupings.

According to SAMHSA, co-occurring psychiatric disorders are common among men. One study found that 55% of the men who identified as having a substance abuse problem also experienced MENtal HEALth problems.

**How old were you when you were introduced to a substance?**

**How often do you use substances?**

**Have you been told you are different when on a substance than when you are sober?**

Do you think the media displays substance use too much?

Do you think all substances are bad?

Do you have a substance of choice?

Did you research that substance?

How do you prevent addiction?

*Express it on the next page...*

# Write it out, MAN! - Substance Use

_____
_____
_____
_____
_____
_____
_____
_____
_____
_____
_____
_____
_____
_____
_____
_____
_____
_____
_____
_____
_____
_____
_____
_____
_____

## *Draw it out, MAN! - Substance Use*

## Lifestyle

This is the way of living for individuals, families (households), or societies. Lifestyles are expressed in both work and leisure behavior patterns, in activities, attitudes, interests, opinions, values, and allocation of income. Lifestyle reflects the self-image as well as self-concept. In return, this is how people share themselves and believe they are seen by the others. Lifestyle is a composite of motivations, needs, and wants and is influenced by factors such as culture, family, reference groups, and social class.

**How does your lifestyle coexist with others?**

**Do others' lifestyles affect you in any way?**

**What are some interesting points of your lifestyle?**

**If you had to change something in your lifestyle, what would it be?**

**How important is a HEALthy lifestyle to you?**

*Express it on the next page...*

# Write it out, MAN! - Lifestyle

## Draw it out, MAN! - Lifestyle

## Cope

This is a fundamental part of life! Coping is the ability to deal with things, whether negative or positive. It is the way behavior is processed when dealing with stresses of life. The behaviors can occur both internally or externally. When you implement cognitive and behavioral strategies that help you deal with stressful situations, this is called coping.

Sometimes, we need to cope with things that happen to us. Then, there are other times we must cope with things that happen within us. These events may entail us to deal with both internal and external demands.

**Internal Example -** Dealing with a sickness or illness, you find ways to get through.

**External Example -** Losing a job, you find ways to continue to push and find another job.


**What is coping to you?**

**How well do you cope to situations?**

**Are you able to cope and move into HEALing?**

**List five internal situations you had to cope to a situation:**

**List external situations where you had to cope to a situation:**


*Express it on the next page...*

## Write it out, MAN! - Cope

_____

_____

_____

_____

_____

_____

_____

_____

_____

_____

_____

_____

_____

_____

_____

_____

_____

_____

_____

_____

_____

_____

_____

_____

_____

_____

_____

_____

## *Draw it out, MAN! - Cope*

## *Coping Skills/Strategies*

Hopefully you learned previously that coping consists of characteristics and different behavioral patterns that enhance the ability to adapt and move forward in situations. There are positive coping skills as well as negative ones.

| Negative Coping Skills | Positive Coping Skills |
|---|---|
| Using drugs | Writing, Drawing, Painting, Photography, Dancing |
| Drinking alcohol excessively | Take a walk, or go for a drive |
| Engaging in self-mutilation | Role-play challenging |
| Avoiding your problems | Write a list of strengths |
| Being in denial | |

**What are your current coping skills?**

**Do you engage in negative coping skills?**

**Do your current coping skills assist you in your time of need?**

*Express it on the next page...*

## Write it out, MAN! - Positive Coping Skills/Strategies

_____

_____

_____

_____

_____

_____

_____

_____

_____

_____

_____

_____

_____

_____

_____

_____

_____

_____

_____

_____

_____

_____

_____

_____

_____

_____

## Draw it out, MAN! - Positive Coping Skills/Strategies

## *Write it out, MAN! - Negative Coping Skills/Strategies*

_____
_____
_____
_____
_____
_____
_____
_____
_____
_____
_____
_____
_____
_____
_____
_____
_____
_____
_____
_____
_____
_____
_____
_____
_____

*Draw it out, MAN! - Negative Coping Skills/Strategies*

## *Emotions*

According to many in society, MEN often feel that they need to be strong and refrain from showing their emotions. Many MEN believe that they have to be this way and provide for their loved ones, so it is not appropriate to express their emotions. This behavior is reinforced as a stereotype by many cultures in today's society. The "heroic" MAN and the "macho" MAN are often represented in popular culture - Fearless, resourceful, stoic, and usually facing adversity alone. These characters tell us a lot about what is considered to be ideal MAN behavior.

In most instances, MEN may feel uncomfortable talking to someone about their emotional state. This often leads to frustration in relationships in the home, work, school and community. Most cannot express their needs, fears and grief outside of being embarrassed or feeling inadequate. Positive things occur when one can express emotions in a healthy way.

**The common emotions shared by MEN:**

- Sadness
- Anger
- Happiness
- Fear
- Shame
- ExciteMENt
- Anxiety

**What healthy emotions do you display?**

What negative emotions you display?

Do you agree with society view of MEN and emotions?

How many emotions can you add to the four?

What is your favorite emotion?

*Express it on the next page...*

# *Write it out, MAN! - Emotions*

_____
_____
_____
_____
_____
_____
_____
_____
_____
_____
_____
_____
_____
_____
_____
_____
_____
_____
_____
_____
_____
_____
_____
_____
_____
_____
_____
_____
_____

*Draw it out, MAN! - Emotions*

## *HEALing*

True HEALing is a much-needed process of repairing what has been damaged or altered in an irregular way. This can be an unbalanced reaction in your life, whether MENtally or physically. This is a journey in itself and takes much practice. Once the process starts, one can be well rounded for their family, friends and coworkers. Many use massages, exercise, meditation, yoga, and various forms of art therapy, to name a few, in order to HEAL.

**How do you HEAL yourself?**

**Do you feel broken or ill?**

**Do you believe in energy?**

**Do you believe HEALing is beneficial?**

**What are the benefits of HEALing?**

**Are people around you practicing HEALing?**

*Express it on the next page...*

## *Write it out, MAN! - HEALing*

_____
_____
_____
_____
_____
_____
_____
_____
_____
_____
_____
_____
_____
_____
_____
_____
_____
_____
_____
_____
_____
_____
_____
_____
_____
_____
_____
_____

# Draw it out, MAN! - HEALing

## Head of Household

Technically, this is a filing status for individual taxpayers in many states. But most of society views this as a MAN's role in the home. Regardless of finances, the pressure is on a MAN to be the "head." It is often expressed in religion, the workplace, and many other entities of life.

**Have you ever heard this term?**

**What does "head of household" mean to you?**

**Do you have to lead your home?**

**Is there pressure to lead your home?**

**Talk about your thoughts on being the head of the household...**

*Express it on the next page...*

## Write it out, MAN! - Head of Household

_____
_____
_____
_____
_____
_____
_____
_____
_____
_____
_____
_____
_____
_____
_____
_____
_____
_____
_____
_____
_____
_____
_____
_____

# Draw it out, MAN! - Head of Household

## Feelings

Earlier we learned what emotions were. Feelings are an experience of emotions. In many cases, it's our feelings that determine whether we are expressing emotions such as happy, sad, excited, or frustrated. Our feelings motivate us to do things. Our feelings about the world are heavily influenced by our past experiences.

Some say feelings are physical and emotions are MENtal, others are confident it's the other way around.

**What do you think about feelings?**

**What are your favorite feelings?**

**What are you feeling now?**

**How do you express your feelings to others?**

**Are your feelings easy to read?**

**Are you afraid of judgement when expressing feelings?**

*Express it on the next page...*

## *Write it out, MAN! - Feelings*

_____
_____
_____
_____
_____
_____
_____
_____
_____
_____
_____
_____
_____
_____
_____
_____
_____
_____
_____
_____
_____
_____
_____
_____
_____
_____
_____
_____

## Draw it out, MAN! - Feelings

## Family

Besides sharing the same DNA, this is where most people acquire basic socialization skills for life. Family can be comprised of many different constructs. Sadly, research suggests that there have been more single parent households than traditional two-parent households. Some members of society think there is a linkage between an individuals' family structure and their behaviors (good and bad). When it comes to family, two things for certain will happen, you will work to keep the cycle going, or work tirelessly to break the cycle. Family is supposed to be one of the first lines of support systems. Family can also give you predisposed issues with your health, whether mentally, physically, or emotionally.

**How would you describe your family structure?**

**Does your family support you?**

**What would you change about your current family dynamic?**

**What will your future family look like?**

**What traits would you pass down?**

**What traits would you avoid passing down?**

*Express it on the next page...*

# *Write it out, MAN! - Family*

_____

_____

_____

_____

_____

_____

_____

_____

_____

_____

_____

_____

_____

_____

_____

_____

_____

_____

_____

# Draw it out, MAN! - Family

## Love

This is probably one of the most challenging things in life! When it comes to love, there are many factors that are incorporated. Love connects the emotional and mental states, from the most inspirational virtue or good habit, the deepest interpersonal affection, and to the simplest pleasures. Some will also say that love is a mixture, or a collection, of different traits. According to the Greeks, *Eros* is sexual or passionate love, and is the type most akin to our modern construct of romantic love. *Philia*, or friendship, is shared goodwill - You help me and I will help you. *Storge* is the love between parents and their children. *Agape* is universal love, such as the love for strangers, nature, or your higher power in religion. *Ludus* is playful or uncommitted love. *Pragma* is a kind of practical love founded on reason to stay with someone. *Philautia* is self-love, which can be healthy or unhealthy. There are many types of love and many definitions, I tried to narrow it down to make it easy.

**What do you think love is?**

**Have you ever been in love?**

**What kind of love do you give?**

**What do you love about yourself?**

**Do you feel loved?**

**How do you show love?**

**List five things you love:**

## Express it on the next page...

# Write it out, MAN! - Love

_____

_____

_____

_____

_____

_____

_____

_____

_____

_____

_____

_____

_____

_____

_____

_____

_____

_____

_____

## Draw it out, MAN! – Love

## *Selfcare*

There is still some confusion about this being a *selfish* act. Just a reminder... it's OK to take care of yourself! Spend more time being as kind to yourself as you would be to others. This is for *your* recovery. Self-care is any activity that should be deliberately done in order to take care of our MENtal, emotional, and physical health. Good self-care is key to an improved mood and reducing other potential health issues. It can also improve the relationship with your self and others.

**Do you think selfcare is selfish? Why or why not?**

**What do you do for your own selfcare?**

**How important is selfcare to you?**

**What was your last selfcare activity?**

**What is your next selfcare activity?**

*Express it on the next page...*

## *Write it out, MAN! - Selfcare*

_____

_____

_____

_____

_____

_____

_____

_____

_____

_____

_____

_____

_____

_____

_____

_____

_____

_____

_____

_____

## Draw it out, MAN! - Selfcare

## *Forgiveness*

Forgiving is to release the anger that you have been holding on to. You are not required to forget, or reconnect, with the person who wronged you. When you forgive, it's for you and you alone. Forgiveness is extremely important for your mental health. In many cases, this can propel you forward rather than keeping you emotionally engaged in an injustice or trauma. When one forgives, it can elevate moods, enhance optimism, and protect you against [your own] anger. Imagine reducing stress, anxiety, and depression just by getting the weight from others' improper actions off you.

**Is it important for you to forgive?**

**How often do you forgive?**

**Can you forgive and forget?**

**How did you feel after you forgave?**

**Did someone forgive you?**

**When was the last time you had to forgive someone?**

**Name a situation(s) that was difficult to forgive:**

*Express it on the next page...*

*Write it out, MAN! - Forgiveness*

## Draw it out, MAN! - Forgiveness

## Relationships

This is the strong bond with someone who hopefully sees you as you see them. Relationships can be complex. On average, MEN and woMEN often have a difficult time understanding each other and ignore the basis of communication. The keys to a successful relationship are to continually work at not only making the other person happy, but making yourself happy. Some woMEN would say that MEN are often more inclined to ignore issues that arise in their relationships, so it is important for MEN to make an effort to process with them.

**Are you in a relationship now?**

**What is your ideal relationship?**

**How comfortable are you with taking accountability?**

**Are you willing to commit?**

**What are your biggest fears in a relationship?**

**What are some old habits you're going to leave in the past?**

**How much time do you take in-between relationships?**

*Express it on the next page...*

# *Write it out, MAN! - Relationships*

_____

_____

_____

_____

_____

_____

_____

_____

_____

_____

_____

_____

_____

_____

_____

_____

_____

_____

_____

_____

_____

# *Draw it out, MAN! - Relationships*

## Crying

Based on society and the media, MEN aren't supposed to cry - Probably one of the saddest misconceptions today. Just a reminder, this is a normal human action, not a gender specific action for MEN and woMEN separately. Crying can be triggered by many different emotions. When you cry, you can release multiple types of tears.

The three types of tears are:

- **Reflex tears**
- **Continuous tears**
- **Emotional tears**

The benefits of reflex tears are to clear debris, like smoke and dust, from your eyes. Continuous tears are those that lubricate our eyes and help protect them from infection. Emotional tears are the ones we use to display our feelings and they have many health benefits. Endorphins are the feel-good chemicals that are released when one cries. Releasing these chemicals can help ease both physical and emotional pain.

**Do you feel that MEN aren't supposed to cry?**

**Growing up, were you told not to cry?**

**How do you feel about crying?**

**Is there a difference in boys/MEN crying than a girl/woMAN crying?**

**When was the last time you cried?**

**Do you cry in front of people?**

### Express it on the next page...

## *Write it out, MAN! - Crying*

_____

_____

_____

_____

_____

_____

_____

_____

_____

_____

_____

_____

_____

_____

_____

_____

_____

_____

_____

_____

## Draw it out, MAN! - Crying

## Ego

This is a strong portion of the human personality which is experienced as the "self" or "I". This interaction participates with your internal thoughts and external world through perception. Between you and I, the ego can be held responsible for many negative traits in our day to day. This is often disguised as striving to be right, always wanting to be superior over others, and a host of thoughts.

**Do you have an ego?**

**How do you define your ego?**

**Has your ego disrupted your day?**

**Do you think your ego impacts you or others negatively?**

**Can you take a backseat to your ego?**

**Can you spot ego in others?**

**Do you think having an ego gets in the way of progress?**

*Express it on the next page...*

## Write it out, MAN! - Ego

_____
_____
_____
_____
_____
_____
_____
_____
_____
_____
_____
_____
_____
_____
_____
_____
_____
_____
_____
_____
_____

*Draw it out, MAN! - Ego*

## Society's Perception of You

1.  If I ask ten random people what they think of you, what would they say?
2.  How would your parent(s) describe you?
3.  How would your teacher(s) describe you?
4.  How would your sibling(s) describe you?
5.  How would your boss/coworker(s) describe you?
6.  Would their answers make you evaluate yourself?
7.  Make a list of how you would describe yourself.
8.  Did any of your thoughts match the thoughts of those above persons' description of you?
9.  Does the perception of others bother you?
10. Do you try to change the things others don't like about you?

*Express it on the next page...*

## Write it out, MAN! - Society's Perception of You

_____

_____

_____

_____

_____

_____

_____

_____

_____

_____

_____

_____

_____

_____

_____

_____

_____

_____

_____

_____

_____

# *Draw it out, MAN! – Society's Perception of You*

## *Your Perception of You*

Describe yourself in 20 words or less (or draw a pic) on the next couple pages and then answer the following:

1. How tall are you?
2. How much do you weigh?
3. What do you see when you look in the mirror?
4. I am...?
5. I can do better at...?
6. I am good at...?
7. I feel good when...?
8. I smile the hardest when...?
9. I get upset when...?
10. I like to...?
11. What kind of king would you be?

*Express it on the next page...*

# *Write it out, MAN! - Your Perception of You*

_____

_____

_____

_____

_____

_____

_____

_____

_____

_____

_____

_____

_____

_____

_____

_____

_____

_____

_____

_____

# Draw it out, MAN! - Your Perception of You

## *Happiness*

This is so subjective! The things that make me happy may not be the same for you. Happiness is the pure joy within self. Happiness has even been linked to a longer lifespan as well as a higher quality of life and well-being. As one gets older, I think we rate happiness more important than other desirable personal outcomes, such as obtaining wealth, acquiring material goods, and getting into heaven. Happiness can be altered by life circumstances, achievements, marital status, social relationships, even our neighbors.

**Are you happy now?**

**When was the last time you were happy?**

**What do you need to be happy?**

**Do you make others happy?**

**Do material things make you happy?**

**When are you at your happiest?**

*Express it on the next page...*

# Write it out, MAN! - Happiness

_____

_____

_____

_____

_____

_____

_____

_____

_____

_____

_____

_____

_____

_____

_____

_____

_____

_____

_____

_____

## Draw it out, MAN! - Happiness

## *AttachMENt*

I consider this a strong bond and/or connection to something. This bond can be emotional and often forms between you and the people that assist with your primary needs. As you get older, this becomes the engine for ensuring that social, emotional, and cognitive development coexists.

**What material thing(s) are you attached to?**

**What person(s) in your life are you attached to most?**

**What does healthy attachment look like?**

**Have you ever been attached to the wrong thing?**

*Express it on the next page...*

# *Write it out, MAN! - AttachMENt*

---

---

---

---

---

---

---

---

---

---

---

---

---

---

---

---

---

---

---

# Draw it out, MAN! - AttachMENt

## *Triggers*

Think of these as reminders, triggers often give us a reason to respond, whether positive or negative. These small things, or big things in some cases, can stimulate our senses, such as recalling a smell, sound, or sight from a past event that occurred. Knowing your triggers can assist you a great deal in your day-to-day life with school, work, and family. If you can identify your triggers, you could solve potential issues before they arise. A trigger can be a cue that prompts an increase in symptoms or assists in preventing addiction and/or distress and adverse behaviors.

**Example** - If you are depressed, being able to identify what makes you feel depressed helps prevent symptoms the symptoms. Triggers may be financial, being left alone, lack of support etc.

**Example** - Substance use, knowing when your substance use increases is part of knowing your triggers. This type of trigger can be hanging around certain friends, increased stress, arguments etc.


**What are your triggers?**

**How long was it before you were able to identify your triggers?**

**Now that you know your triggers, how does this assist you?**

**What can/do you do when you are triggered?**


## *Express it on the next page...*

## Write it out, MAN! - Triggers

_____

_____

_____

_____

_____

_____

_____

_____

_____

_____

_____

_____

_____

_____

_____

_____

_____

_____

## Draw it out, MAN! - Triggers

## MAN Cave

Every MAN needs one at some point! This is the place you can escape to that's drama and stress free, but still close to home. The MAN cave is an important place to establish in order to ground your self - A place where you can return to focus. The MAN cave provides a place to temporarily get away from the pressures of life. You, like woMEN, also need to decompress so that there is emotional energy left over for family life, work life and self. This is an essential, MEN-Only space to retreat to:

- Meditate
- Watch sports
- Create
- Think
- Hang with the guys

**Do you currently have a MAN cave?**

**Describe your MAN cave? If you don't have one, describe what it would look like?**

**How big is it, colors, items inside?**

**What would you do in your MAN cave?**

*Express it on the next page...*

## Write it out, MAN! - Man Cave

---

---

---

---

---

---

---

---

---

---

---

---

---

---

---

---

---

---

---

---

---

## Draw it out, MAN! - Man Cave

## HEALthy

Often times, the term *HEALthy* is only associated with physical HEALth – "Do you have any aches or pains?" Rarely do people associate *HEALthy* with the emotional and MENtal areas. In actuality, *HEALthy* refers to a state of complete emotional and physical well-being. Most commonly, you hear about physical HEALth and the bodily functions that are working at peak performance due to not only an absence of disease, but also to regular exercise, balanced nutrition, and adequate rest. But there is also MENtal health, which refers to a person's emotional, social, and psychological imprint. MENtal HEALth is just as important to a full and active lifestyle as physical HEALth. Sadly, there is no abundance of MEN attending doctor's appointments unless they're in excruciating pain or can see blood! The numbers are even lower for MEN seeing MENtal HEALth providers. In good practice, a yearly examination should take place; six months is even better.

**Do you consider MENtal HEALth and physical HEALth equally important?**

**Are you willing to go to the doctor/therapist more?**

**What can you do to improve your physical HEALth?**

**What can you do to improve your MENtal HEALth?**

**When was the last time you obtained a physical or got a checkup from your PCP?**

**Have you ever seen a therapist or counselor for your MENtal HEALth?**

*Express it on the next page...*

## Write it out, MAN! - HEALthy

_____

_____

_____

_____

_____

_____

_____

_____

_____

_____

_____

_____

_____

_____

_____

_____

_____

_____

## Draw it out, MAN! - HEALthy

## Deep Breathing

I think that this is a greatly underestimated lifesaver! A few deep breaths, using this exercise in a time of crisis or distress can assist you in regaining your focus and formulating a plan. Deep breathing is breathing in a way that completely fills your lungs while inhaling and completely emptying the lungs on the exhale. So this is what you do: Get comfortable, breathe in through your nose, let your belly fill with air, breathe out through your nose or breath out through your mouth using pursed lips. As you breathe in, feel your belly rise. As you breathe out, feel your belly lower. Take three more full, deep breaths. Lastly, repeat all over! Breathe fully into your belly as it rises and falls with your breath.

**Deep breathing interventions have lifestyle benefits:**

- ❖ Increase in confidence
- ❖ Decrease in anxiety
- ❖ Better Sleep
- ❖ Improvement in mood

**Have you done deep breathing before?**

**Are you willing to try it?**

**Do you think was effective?**

**How do you feel after trying it?**

**Besides deep breathing, what strategies can you do?**

**Give ten deep breaths now:**

## Express it on the next page...

# *Write it out, MAN! - Deep Breathing*

---
---
---
---
---
---
---
---
---
---
---
---
---
---
---
---
---
---
---
---

## *Draw it out, MAN! - Deep Breathing*

## Children

They are the influential little ones that we have to set a positive example for. The earlier we start; the better society and its norms will become. What if we set the parameters for what's acceptable and unacceptable in regards to boys/MEN? Imagine it being OK for the little boy to want to bake opposed to playing a sport or video game. Imagine if that young boy is embraced when he falls and hurts his knee like the young lady is. Think about if more empathy and sympathy were geared towards the HEALthy expression of feelings at a young age. Children follow the examples of adults, whether good or bad.

**Do you think children should be guided towards being free?**

**Do you think inclusion helps or hurts children?**

**How do you feel when a boy doesn't want to do masculine things?**

**Should boys and girls be raised differently?**

**Should boys cry?**

**Do children have more issues today with the addition of social media?**

**How can we protect our children?**

*Express it on the next page...*

## Write it out, MAN! - Children

_____

_____

_____

_____

_____

_____

_____

_____

_____

_____

_____

_____

_____

_____

_____

_____

_____

_____

_____

_____

_____

_____

## Draw it out, MAN! - Children

## *Sadness*

This is a collection of "down" feelings or emotions. Sadness comes when one has thoughts of disadvantage, loss, despair, grief, helplessness, disappointment and/or sorrow. Being sad for extended periods of time can lead to depression. Not being able to express sadness in a HEALthy way can cause impairments and create other issues.

**What makes you sad?**

**When was the last time you were sad more than a week?**

**What do you do when you are sad?**

**How often do you experience sadness?**

**How do you assist others when they are sad?**

*Express it on the next page...*

## *Write it out, MAN! - Sadness*

_____

_____

_____

_____

_____

_____

_____

_____

_____

_____

_____

_____

_____

_____

_____

_____

_____

_____

_____

# Draw it out, MAN! - Sadness

## Support

I believe that this is one of the most important aspects in a few different areas of life. If one is in recovery, support is key. If one is dealing with an issue or illness, support is very necessary. Support is a collection of people or resources you can rely on in time of need. When one receives support from their friends, family, or peers', that person will likely prosper more in what they set out to do than if they didn't have that support.

**What does support look like to you?**

**Do you need more support?**

**Who is your current support system?**

**Do you support your friends, family or peers?**

**Name a situation that you required support and didn't receive it:**

**Name a situation where you display an abundance of support to someone:**

*Express it on the next page...*

## *Write it out, MAN! - Support*

_____

_____

_____

_____

_____

_____

_____

_____

_____

_____

_____

_____

_____

_____

_____

_____

_____

_____

_____

# Draw it out, MAN! - Support

## MANhood

I define this as a collection of experiences that a male possesses. Each boy, in his adolescence, needs to go through certain experiences in order to become a full-grown MAN. These challenges will then dictate a uniqueness to HIM specifically. MANhood itself can be subjective in which qualities it requires or what one must have. One can take care of his family and be considered as having reached MANhood, while one can have multiple women and also be labeled as reaching MANhood. Maturity plays a big part in this journey.

**How do you define MANhood?**

**What qualities are possessed to determine MANhood?**

**Do you think this is learned or given to all MEN at a certain age?**

**Are you in your MANhood stage of life?**

**What decides your MANhood?**

*Express it on the next page...*

## Write it out, MAN! - MANhood

_____

_____

_____

_____

_____

_____

_____

_____

_____

_____

_____

_____

_____

_____

_____

_____

_____

_____

_____

## Draw it out, MAN! - MANhood

## Resilience

On the other side of trauma and negative experiences in life, there is resilience. When faced with issues, one has to be able to recover quickly or adjust in order to prevent further harm. Think of it as finding a way to rise up in the midst of tough situations. Some will not let difficulties or failure overcome them.

**Do you practice resiliency?**

**Name a time where you had to be resilient?**

**What are benefits of being resilient?**

**How can you increase your resilience?**

**Do you think we all have resiliency?**

*Express it on the next page...*

## *Write it out, MAN! - Resilience*

_____

_____

_____

_____

_____

_____

_____

_____

_____

_____

_____

_____

_____

_____

_____

_____

_____

_____

_____

_____

# *Draw it out, MAN! - Resilience*

## Diet

From a nutrition standpoint, this requires ingestion and absorption of different vitamins, minerals, amino acids and others sources including protein and essential fatty acids. Our body then turns this into food energy in the form of carbohydrates, protein, and fat. HEALth issues have been easily linked to its relationship with food and diet. It is important for MEN to do all they can to reduce the risk of some chronic diseases. A HEALthy diet can increase endurance. It can also help your overall MENtal HEALth. Did you know that obesity puts you more at risk for things like diabetes, high cholesterol, heart attack, and high blood pressure? The risk of diabetes can make you lose your legs, if not prevented. High cholesterol levels and high blood pressure cause heart attacks or strokes. Many of these diseases can be prevented with a proper diet.

**Have you tried to diet before?**

**Are you open to trying a diet?**

**What is your diet?**

**If you could eliminate or change something in your diet what would it be?**

**How do you feel while dieting in comparison to not dieting?**

*Express it on the next page...*

## *Write it out, MAN! - Diet*

_____
_____
_____
_____
_____
_____
_____
_____
_____
_____
_____
_____
_____
_____
_____
_____
_____
_____
_____
_____
_____

## Draw it out, MAN! - Diet

## *Intentions*

I challenge you to do something each day to demonstrate your commitment to your intentions. Some people lack "follow through." When you set intentions, make a strong plan to live up to them. Previously, we discussed goals, but intentions are different. What really sets an intention apart from a goal or a want is how an intention comes from dwelling on the present, whereas a goal is more of a future projection. Intentions are not proclamations; they're more of a guideline for what you want to do. Having good intentions can have a lasting effect on nurturing your consciousness. When you actively do that, you create the power to significantly raise your awareness. When you set an intention, you don't have to worry about your actions or the responses after. In theory, setting firm and righteous intentions will create righteous actions.

**What are your thoughts on intentions?**

**How are your goals different?**

**What do you intend to do within the next week or so?**

**Display five intentions you plan to do within the next 90 days:**

*Express it on the next page...*

## *Write it out, MAN! - Intentions*

_____

_____

_____

_____

_____

_____

_____

_____

_____

_____

_____

_____

_____

_____

_____

_____

_____

_____

_____

# Draw it out, MAN! - Intentions

## Conflict

When one or more people have a disagreement, we can view this as conflict. This can be met with hostility or gentleness. The elements involved in the conflict have diverse sets of principles and values, thus allowing such a struggle to arise. Conflict comes naturally; the way one handles it is where many have issues. Where you may just want to talk it out and communicate, the other person may want to get physical or become irate. It's not uncommon for the clashing of thoughts and ideas to be destructive if left uncontrolled.

**How do you handle conflict?**

**When was your last conflict?**

**How would you prevent conflict?**

**What's a conflict you wish you would NOT have engaged in?**

**What's a conflict you wish you would've have engaged in?**

*Express it on the next page...*

# *Write it out, MAN! - Conflict*

_____

_____

_____

_____

_____

_____

_____

_____

_____

_____

_____

_____

_____

_____

_____

_____

_____

_____

_____

## Draw it out, MAN! - Conflict

## *Stress*

Here is a secret... Stress is normal. The mismanagement of stress is the issue. When it is not controlled properly, we react in ways that aren't HEALthy to our overall state. Our body changes physically, MENtally, and/or emotionally. You can experience stress from your environment, school, finances, work, family, your body, and your thoughts to name a few. If it weren't for keeping us alert, motivated, and ready to avoid danger, stress would cause many people to have other issues.

Stress that continues without a break can lead to a condition called distress. This is a negative reaction that our body displays in its internal balance or equilibrium, leading to physical symptoms such as headaches, an upset stomach, elevated blood pressure, chest pain, sexual dysfunction, and problems sleeping.

**What causes you to stress?**

**What are your stress reduction techniques?**

**How can you prevent stress?**

**Do you have any of those above symptoms when you're too stressed?**

*Express it on the next page...*

## Write it out, MAN! - Stress

_____

_____

_____

_____

_____

_____

_____

_____

_____

_____

_____

_____

_____

_____

_____

_____

_____

_____

_____

_____

_____

*Draw it out, MAN! - Stress*

## Confidence

Being confident involves having a realistic sense of your capabilities and then linking them to feeling secure in that knowledge. This is a two-way dynamic in most cases when viewed by others' perception of how you display your confidence. Too much confidence can make you appear cocky and arrogant. The other side is, if you are underestimating your abilities, you may lose out on opportunities.

Luckily for us, this ability that can be acquired and improved over time. The characteristics of confidence vary from person to person.

**Do you have confidence in yourself?**

**Do you have a balance of confidence and arrogance?**

**How do you increase your confidence?**

**What areas do you lack confidence?**

**What areas do you want to gain confidence in?**

*Express it on the next page...*

## Write it out, MAN! - Confidence

_____

_____

_____

_____

_____

_____

_____

_____

_____

_____

_____

_____

_____

_____

_____

_____

_____

_____

_____

_____

*Draw it out, MAN! - Confidence*

## *Attention*

Our minds have a way of focusing on a task or job. I would describe *attention* as the cognitive process of selectively concentrating on one main aspect of a specified task while ignoring or limiting your responses to other things. Observing the cognitive processes that are associated with our mind, such as decision-making, memory, emotion, and concentration, attention is measured to be one of the most concrete due to how we perceive things afterwards. Attention can be broken down into approximately five different styles:

**Focused attention -** This is the skill to directly reply to specific stimuli using your senses (visual, auditory or tactile). Example, when you are listening to music, you turn it up to catch exactly what the artist said, tuning out the beat, the background noise, etc. Just the specific reference you're looking for.

**Sustained attention -** The ability to maintain a steady behavioral response during a continuous and repetitive activity. Example, you're in a lecture and you focus directly on the speaker until his/her time is up.

**Selective attention -** This type of attention is the ability to maintain a behavioral or cognitive set in the face of disrupting or opposing stimuli. Example, you are exercising "freedom from distractibility" you're watching a movie and someone continues to walk across the television but you continue to listen and look around them without missing the plot.

**Alternating attention -** This refers to the likelihood that you have mental flexibility that will allow you to shift your focus and attention between tasks while having different cognitive necessities. Example, you're driving a car, you have to steer, use the peddles, as well as look out the windows for safety.

**Divided attention -** This attention style is the skill to respond simultaneously to multiple demands at once, similar to alternating but at a higher level. Example, you're cooking dinner, reading a recipe and talking to another person in the kitchen. Your focus is divided almost equally on each task because they can sustain without you individually.

**Are you easily distracted?**

**How well is your attention and attentiveness?**

**Which stage or stages of attention to you use the most?**

**Which stage or you use the least?**

**What area of the day are you most focused (morning, evening or night)?**

**What holds your focus more (work/school, friends/family, television/radio or something else)?**

*Express it on the next page...*

## Write it out, MAN! - Attention

# Draw it out, MAN! - Attention

## MENtal HEALth

This is a collection of our being that includes emotional, psychological, and social well-being. These things act as one to help us determine how we process stress, relationships with others, and make choices. Over the course of our lives, it is safe to say that we will have some form of involvement with MENtal HEALth. This can show in your thinking, mood, and behavior.

Three main factors contribute to MENtal HEALth:

- Biological factors, such as genes or brain chemistry
- Life experiences, such as trauma or abuse
- Family history of MENtal HEALth problems

**How is your MENtal HEALth?**

**What do you do to keep your MENtal HEALth intact?**

**Is there a history of MENtal HEALth issues in your family?**

**What do you do to maintain good MENtal HEALth?**

**What would you do if you needed assistance with improving your MENtal HEALth?**

**Do you judge those with challenges in their MENtal HEALth?**

**Are you an advocate for MENtal HEALth?**

*Express it on the next page...*

## Write it out, MAN! - MENtal HEALth

_____

_____

_____

_____

_____

_____

_____

_____

_____

_____

_____

_____

_____

_____

_____

_____

_____

_____

_____

_____

# Draw it out, MAN! - MENtal HEALth

## Social Media

It's a new age, and everything these days are online! This can be a bad thing and/or a good thing. Social media should be used in moderation. If you look at the addiction criteria, social media is a form of addiction. It has some of our friends neglecting their personal life, MENtal preoccupation, trying hard to find a form of escapism, mood modifying experiences, tolerance, and concealing the addictive behavior by being online. Many can see that social media is encouraging people to form and cherish artificial bonds over actual friendships. Increased feelings of jealousy can make a person want to make his or her own life appear to look better and post jealousy-inducing content of their own, in an endless circle of one-upping and feeling jealous. Not to mention, cyber bullying is one factor why social media should be used in moderation.

**How do you use social media?**

**What social media platforms do you spend the most time on?**

**Do you think it is addictive?**

**Have you expressed envy or had envy come your way from a post?**

**How do you limit your use of social media?**

**Do you think social media is hurting our culture?**

**Are you mindful of what you post and follow?**

*Express it on the next page...*

# Write it out, MAN! - Social Media

_____

_____

_____

_____

_____

_____

_____

_____

_____

_____

_____

_____

_____

_____

_____

_____

_____

_____

_____

_____

_____

# Draw it out, MAN! - Social Media

## *Peer Pressure*

Yes, sadly it still exists. It is important to manage peer pressure without losing your own identity. There are healthy ways to interact with your friends and peers. However, time and time again, some may succumb to negative interactions and become a victim of depression, violence, anxiety and various other MENtal disorders. Once you increase confidence and self-esteem, it becomes a tool and making your own choices becomes easier.

**Has peer pressure affected or impacted you in anyway?**

**Do you have confidence and self-esteem to avoid certain situations?**

**Have you ever pressured others?**

**Are you a leader or follower?**

**What does peer pressure mean to you?**

**What would you do if you see others being pressured?**

**List five examples of how you avoided negative peer pressure:**

*Express it on the next page...*

# *Write it out, MAN! - Peer Pressure*

_____

_____

_____

_____

_____

_____

_____

_____

_____

_____

_____

_____

_____

_____

_____

_____

_____

_____

_____

_____

_____

_____

_____

## Draw it out, MAN! - Peer Pressure

## Leadership

You are a natural born leader! Whether the opportunity is presented or not is another story. You probably started early, like a captain of a sports team or line leader in school, and the attributes stuck with you. Successful leaders also tend to embody integrity and emotional intelligence, characteristics that support the forming of a fair, balanced, and satisfied professional team. These values are associated with a strong hierarchical structure. Some MEN believe that such an approach ensures effective delegation of responsibilities and tasks.

**What is a good leader?**

**Do you think you are a leader?**

**Do you like the role of a leader?**

**Are you an effective leader?**

**What qualities of leadership do you possess?**

**When was the last time you had to lead?**

**What do you do when you are a subordinate to a bad leader?**

*Express it on the next page...*

# Write it out, MAN! - Leadership

_____

_____

_____

_____

_____

_____

_____

_____

_____

_____

_____

_____

_____

_____

_____

_____

_____

_____

_____

_____

_____

_____

## Draw it out, MAN! - Leadership

## Sports

Sports play a vital role in many people's lives. This was more than likely the first time you had to compete. They also probably serve as a way for you to relax and take your mind off a rough day. Sports are an outlet as well as a form of exercise. Playing sports has demonstrated a link between MENtal HEALth and happiness; probably because of the endorphins that are triggered. It's not uncommon for us to grow up with a favorite team, or player, and model our likeness after them. Sports can also be beneficial in teaching teamwork and leadership.

**Do you play sports? If so, which ones?**

**Do you think MEN should only play physical, combative sports like basketball, MMA, football and not gymnastics?**

**Do you think sports promote gender equality?**

**Do you use sports as an outlet, whether playing or watching?**

**How has sports helped you?**

**What do you do if you don't play or watch sports?**

**Do you think MEN and woMEN should play sports together?**

*Express it on the next page...*

## *Write it out, MAN! - Sports*

_____

_____

_____

_____

_____

_____

_____

_____

_____

_____

_____

_____

_____

_____

_____

_____

_____

_____

_____

_____

# Draw it out, MAN! - Sports

## Pride

I believe that pride is a fine line between arrogance and humility that is displayed both internally and externally. Pride has a tendency to force us to focus on the disadvantages instead of the advantages, no matter how significant. At any moment, the authentic you, with all of your faults and uncertainties, can be revealed to the world. Pride can cause you to stand in your own way or shelter your true self from being embarrassed. Many have been so self-absorbed that they become self-unaware. When that happens, the egos tend to get damaged. People lose to their insecurities because they have focused so much on falsifying them for the sake of others.

**Do you have pride?**

**Is your pride an issue?**

**What does pride mean to you?**

**How often does your pride get in the way?**

**Have you ever been accused of having an ego or being too prideful?**

**Does your pride let you embrace your insecurities?**

**List a situation where your pride stopped you from accomplishing a task:**

*Express it on the next page...*

## *Write it out, MAN! - Pride*

# Draw it out, MAN! - Pride

## Tough Love

It's been known that girls are nurtured and boys are thrown to the wolves. It's a myth that boys need less love and affection than girls. There are more impactful ways to ensure that a boy/MAN is held responsible for the choices he makes other than belittling or treating him harshly. Society appears to be harder on males so as not to make them soft or turn feminine. The tough love approach should not advocate abuse to males or females for that matter. It should simply teach responsibility by being firm and consistent. I don't see a boy/MAN changing his actions, thoughts, gender or anything else by being embarrassed, shamed, or abused because of his choices.

**What are your thoughts on tough love?**


**Did your guardian use the tough love approach?**

**Do you think males and females should be raised differently?**

**Do you think society frowns upon a MAN getting treated with sensitivity?**

**What are some ways to be firm outside of tough love?**

**Do you use this approach with your children or friends?**

*Express it on the next page...*

# *Write it out, MAN? - Tough Love*

_____

_____

_____

_____

_____

_____

_____

_____

_____

_____

_____

_____

_____

_____

_____

_____

_____

_____

_____

_____

_____

_____

## Draw it out, MAN! - Tough Love

## *Motivation*

This can be considered as the combination of biological, emotional, social, and cognitive forces that activate behaviors and work together. Did you know that dopamine is the chemical that signals the passing of information from one neuron to the next? This is what gives an individual the ability to get things done. When dopamine is released, it soars between the synapse between the first and second neurons. That's a long way of saying what initiates you to get things done. Behaviors are motivated by instincts, which are fixed and inborn patterns of behavior. The drive to get your basic needs met is also a factor for motivation.

**Two types of motivation:**

**Extrinsic motivation** ascends from outside of the rewards such as trophies, money, social recognition, or praise.

**Intrinsic motivation,** on the other hand, arises from within the individual, such as doing a complex journal virtuously for the personal gratification.

**Are you motivated?**

**What is your motivation?**

**How do you stay motivated?**

**How often do you lose motivation?**

**How do find motivation?**

**What is your extrinsic motivation?**

**What is your intrinsic motivation?**

## *Express it on the next page...*

## *Write it out, MAN! - Motivation*

# *Draw it out, MAN! - Motivation*

## MENtality

This is the customary way of being rational, interpreting, and replying to events, practices, and daily things happening that are unusual to a MAN. There is often an arguMENt between mindset and MENtality. On the contrast, mindset has logical reasoning and rationality that will more than likely present arguments with a logical response while MENtality will counter your thoughts with your internal drive and determination that has made the MAN what he is or what he is becoming.

**Example mindset:** "If I lift these weights, I will get bigger and faster. Then I will score more touchdowns or baskets."

**Example MENtality:** Understanding that you were able to run faster and outscore them because you lifted all those weights while they were out partying and not focused.

Like muscles, we must always train our MENtality to make us stronger and overcome each situation. Believe it or not, throughout the course of our lifetime, there will be tests and trials that will either build your MENtality or tear it down.

**Do you see a difference in MENtality and mindset?**

**What is your MENtality?**

**What is your mindset?**

**Can you see the difference from last year until now?**

**What shaped your MENtality, good times or challenging times?**

**What is your MENtality, keep going or give up when you meet resistance?**

How does your MENtality differ now than it did last year?

What's three examples of when your MENtality got you out of a situation?

*Express it on the next page...*

## Write it out, MAN! - MENtality

_____

_____

_____

_____

_____

_____

_____

_____

_____

_____

_____

_____

_____

_____

_____

_____

_____

_____

_____

_____

_____

*Draw it out, MAN! - MENtality*

## Communication

Don't over think this! It is simply how one transfers information from one place, person or group to another. This process has to involve, at a minimum, a sender, a message, and a recipient. Of course, there are group discussions and other ways to communicate. Communication can occur in more than one way at any given time. This can happen with:

**Verbal Communication** - Face-to-face, telephone, radio or television, and other media forms where someone is speaking.

**Nonverbal Communication** - Gestures, how we dress or act, where we stand, to name a few. Many do not give body language its deserving credit, but it is very affective.

**Written Communication** - Letters, e-mails, social media, books, magazines, the Internet, text messaging, and other media forms.

When communicating, ensure that you are clear and concise on what you want the receiver of the message to understand. Communication breaks down when there is an *assumption* that the other person understands us. When communicating, acknowledge the receiver and display understanding, and if either of you do not comprehend the other, then try explaining the message clearer. Effective communication is a continuous process.

**Do you have effective communication?**

**Which way do you like communicating the most (verbal, nonverbal or written)?**

**How often does your communication get mixed up?**

Is it easy for you to communicate your emotions, thoughts and feelings to others?

Would you rather communicate to another MAN or to a woMAN?

What areas of communication can you work on?

Are you good at reading nonverbal communication?

*Express it on the next page...*

## Write it out, MAN! - Communication

_____

_____

_____

_____

_____

_____

_____

_____

_____

_____

_____

_____

_____

_____

_____

_____

_____

_____

_____

_____

_____

_____

# Draw it out, MAN! - Communication

## Negative Cognitions

Remember, if there is a negative, then there is room to make a positive. Negative cognitions are the thoughts we refer to as maladaptive self-assessment, self-defeating, or negative beliefs that were developed from a host of adverse or traumatic life experiences. Your experiences are not who you are, they are what happened to you. You can overcome them! The earlier you address your negative cognitions, the faster you can build resilience. Many of the tools previously identified in this body of work can assist you in that journey.

**Do you persistently have the inability to experience positive emotions?**

**How often do you display negative emotions?**

**Do you have negative beliefs about oneself, others, or the world?**

**Have you ever blocked out/didn't remember important aspects of a traumatic situation?**

**Do you feel you deserve happiness?**

*Express it on the next page...*

# *Write it out, MAN! - Negative Cognitions*

_____

_____

_____

_____

_____

_____

_____

_____

_____

_____

_____

_____

_____

_____

_____

_____

_____

_____

_____

_____

_____

# *Draw it out, MAN! - Negative Cognitions*

## Insecurities

This trait is connected to the questioning of your abilities and/or confidence in a certain area. Being open with discussing your shortcomings or personal worries about not measuring up is often seen as a sign of weakness. In a social setting, you may have been trained to avoid looking vulnerable and displaying emotion. Most of this we discussed in a previous session. Some MEN who are insecure may need constant reassurance of love and their worthiness of it. They may display jealous behaviors and act in anxious and controlling ways to keep people around. A lot of insecure MEN are more likely to be emotionally abusive or manipulative. They need to control their environment and keep anyone from exposing their vulnerability. The fear of rejection by friends, coworkers, peers or family is so strong that they create things to fit in, or embellish things that they think will make them more attractive to others.

- Side Note - Understand that everyone has insecurities; these are, in fact, very normal. The issue becomes how we deal with them. Many try to be healthy and productive, but end up being unhealthy and destructive.

**What, if any, are your insecurities?**

**Do you have fears that you don't want others to know?**

**Have you ever been told you are insecure?**

How often do you celebrate your success?

Do you look for validation from others?

Do you have confidence?

*Express it on the next page...*

## *Write it out, MAN! - Insecurities*

_____

_____

_____

_____

_____

_____

_____

_____

_____

_____

_____

_____

_____

_____

_____

_____

_____

_____

_____

_____

_____

# Draw it out, MAN! - Insecurities

## MEN will be MEN, Boys will be Boys

Doesn't that statement alone sound like an excuse for certain behaviors? It doesn't sound like one has a chance to be different from previous decisions of MEN. It's stereotypically used to explain rowdy or naughty behavior that takes place by males. It doesn't hold individuals responsible for their behavior and choices, but rather infers that all MEN, in fact, feel this way or have these similar actions. Those thoughts in society have led to people thinking that MEN or boys are preprogrammed to act in such ways. This phrase also has a tendency to promote a gender stereotype. Assuming MEN and boys are individuals with their own unique personalities, it promotes the idea that anyone who doesn't live up to this subjective definition of masculinity is abnormal.

**How do you feel about the phrase?**

**Do you feel that it is true or does each male have their own identify?**

**Do you feel boxed in when you hear it?**

**What norms do you exhibit that other MEN or boys seem not to? (sew, bake, do you like pink)**

**Have you, or do you use this phrase as an excuse?**

*Express it on the next page...*

## Write it out, MAN! - MEN will be MEN

---

---

---

---

---

---

---

---

---

---

---

---

---

---

---

---

---

---

# Draw it out, MAN! - Boys will be Boys

## Conflict Resolution

This is the process by which two or more parties reach a peaceful resolution to a dispute. This can be informal or formal for one or more people involved. In some cases, conflict can arise due to the lack of neutrality. Conflicts tend to happen because we interpret what would be most fair to us, and then justify this preference on the bases of fairness while the other person think it should be their way.

**What was your last conflict? Was it resolved peacefully?**

**What do you do to resolve conflicts?**

**Do you inform the other parties involved that a problem exists?**

**How often are you willing to compromise?**

**In what ways to you handle conflicts in positive manners?**

**What ways can you improve how you handle conflicts?**

**Have you had conflict resolution training?**

**What ways can you improve handling conflict?**

*Express it on the next page...*

# *Write it out, MAN! - Conflict Resolution*

_____

_____

_____

_____

_____

_____

_____

_____

_____

_____

_____

_____

_____

_____

_____

_____

_____

_____

_____

_____

_____

_____

_____

# Draw it out, MAN! - Conflict Resolution

## Misogyny

This ideology has caused a lot of issues within society. In some cases, this is stereotypically considered an unconscious hatred that MEN form early in life, often as a result of a trauma involving a woMAN figure that they were linked to trust. That woMAN figure could've been abusive or negligent to this young MAN in his past. Collective group of ladies such as mother, sister, teacher or girlfriend can leave the assumption that all woMEN are the same as the ones who hurt them. This is a society issue, not just a MAN issue. Many are unable to realize that other woMEN can also display traits of misogyny. A lesser known form of misogyny occurs between these woMEN. A woMAN may also look down upon and judge another woMAN for her attire and being an overtly sexual being.

**Are you familiar with misogyny?**

**Do you treat woMEN differently than you treat MEN?**

**How do you reduce misogyny in your circle?**

**What do you do when you encounter yourself or others being misogynist?**

**Do you think woMEN can be a misogynist?**

**What is ways misogyny can be changed by you?**

**Are you harder on woMEN than you are on MEN in the same scenarios?**

*Express it on the next page...*

# Write it out, MAN! - Misogyny

_____

_____

_____

_____

_____

_____

_____

_____

_____

_____

_____

_____

_____

_____

_____

_____

_____

_____

_____

_____

## Draw it out, MAN! - Misogyny

## Masculine/Masculinity

The essence of a MAN... The end, huh? Well not exactly. Traits traditionally viewed as masculine can also be found in woMEN. That's why it is important to not put people in a bubble. Androgyny is the combination of masculine and feminine characteristics into an ambiguous form. Androgyny may be expressed with regard to biological sex, gender identity, gender expression, or sexual identity. If you think about it, masculinity is a social construct based on a set of attributes, behaviors, and roles associated with boys and MEN.

There is an ongoing argument that masculinity is linked to the male body; in this view, masculinity is associated with male genitalia. Many aspects of masculinity assumed to be natural are linguistically and culturally driven. Others have advised that although masculinity can be influenced by biology.

**How do you define masculinity?**

**Do you think only MEN can be masculine?**

**Does culture influence masculinity traits?**

**Do you have to be defined as MANly?**

**Are there specific jobs that MEN should do before a woMAN? (taking out trash, change a tire etc.)**

**Have you encountered a masculine woMAN?**

*Express it on the next page...*

## Write it out, MAN! - Masculine

_____

_____

_____

_____

_____

_____

_____

_____

_____

_____

_____

_____

_____

_____

_____

_____

_____

_____

_____

# *Draw it out, MAN! - Masculine*

## Rape Culture

Many cringe just thinking about this. The environment of rape is prevalent in which sexual violence against victims are normalized and exempt in the media and popular culture. Today, rape culture is perpetuated through the use of a few things MENtioned in this text earlier, to include misogynistic language, anger, the objectification of woMEN's bodies, and the glamorization of sexual violence, thereby forming a society that disregards rights and safety of others. There shouldn't be a common belief proliferated within our society reinforcing blame toward the victim. Individuals who adapt to this mindset are more likely to assume that the victim is responsible for the rape and may perceive that the trauma associated with the rape is less severe or believable. MEN should hold other MEN accountable!

**How do you combat this?**

**Do you avoid using language that objectifies or degrades woMEN or victims?**

**Do you speak out if you hear someone else making an offensive joke or trivializing rape?**

**Do you use sexually explicit jokes?**

**Have you been tolerant of sexual harassment?**

**Do you victim blame?**

*Express it on the next page...*

## Write it out, MAN! - Rape Culture

_____

_____

_____

_____

_____

_____

_____

_____

_____

_____

_____

_____

_____

_____

_____

_____

_____

_____

_____

_____

## *Draw it out, MAN! - Rape Culture*

## Take this time to write a short five to ten sentences on the following:

How would your (parent, classmates, spouse, and/or coworker) describe you when you are upset?

_____

_____

_____

_____

_____

_____

Who would you identify as your support system?

_____

_____

_____

_____

_____

_____

Write something about love:

_____

_____

_____

_____

_____

_____

**What is your plan for selfcare in the next approaching weekend?**

_____
_____
_____
_____
_____
_____

**What does a HEALthy YOU look like?**

_____
_____
_____
_____
_____

**Are you ready to display HEALthy emotions?**

_____
_____
_____
_____
_____

**How would you confront your fears?**

_____
_____
_____
_____
_____
_____

**What advice would you give the future you?**

_____

_____

_____

_____

_____

_____


**What do you wish the old you would've known?**

_____

_____

_____

_____

_____

_____

**Thought of the day:** Take a few minutes to write a quick few words on your day. This can be one word or as many words as you want. Example – "Monday - Tired." "Tuesday – I felt excited at work." "Wednesday - Bored out my mind..."

| Sunday | Monday | Tuesday | Wednesday | Thursday | Friday | Saturday |
|--------|--------|---------|-----------|----------|--------|----------|
|        |        |         |           |          |        |          |
|        |        |         |           |          |        |          |
|        |        |         |           |          |        |          |
|        |        |         |           |          |        |          |
|        |        |         |           |          |        |          |

## *Additional Notes*

# Resources

- Emergency: Dial 9-1-1
- If you or someone you know is in immediate danger, please call 911 or go to your nearest hospital emergency department.
- National Suicide Prevention Lifeline: 1-800-273-TALK (8255)
- Red Nacional de Prevención del Suicidio: 1-888-628-9454
- Veterans Crisis Line: 1-800-273-8255 and Press 1, or text 838255
- Trevor Project (LGBTQ youth): 1-866-488-7386 or text "START" to 678678
- SAMHSA (Substance Abuse & Mental Health Services Administration) 1-800-662-HELP (4357)
- Mental Health America of VA WarmLine: (866) 400-6428
- NAMI National Helpline: 800-950-6264
- Assistance Dogs International: www.assistancedogsinternational.org info@assistancedogsinternational.org + online contact form.
- Champ Dogs: www.champdogs.org, 1-314-653-9466
- Companions for Heroes: companionsforheroes.org, information@companionsforheroes, 1-760-519-7774 (business hours), 1-
- 800-592-1194 (after 4:30 p.m.).
- Heeling Allies Assistance Dogs: www.mentalhealthdogs.org,

- info@mentalhealthdogs.org + online contact form.
- Educating Canines Assisting with Disabilities (ECAD): www.ecad1.org, Email: info@ecad1.org , 1-860-489-6550
- LGBTQ Virginia Sexual & Domestic Violence Action Alliance: 1-866-356-6998.
- National Domestic Violence Hotline: 1-800-799-7233.
- RAINN (Rape< Abuse, Incest National Network): 24/7 help—1-800-656-4673.
- THE LIFELINE 24/7 AT 1-800-273-TALK (8255) OR TEXT 'TALK' to 741741, The Crisis Text Line
- LGBTQ YOUTH: WWW.THETREVORPROJECT.ORG, 1-866-488-7386

## *Who should buy this book/journal?*

**Therapist -** Many therapists enjoy recommending books to their clients to supplement the work they are doing together. We also use books to help ourselves grow as people and practitioners. Remember though that books are never a replacement for real human connection, for supervision and continuing education, or for therapy when it's needed. This is a tool that is helpful for a MAN who is reluctant or has a fear of seeing a therapist face to face. This should be used to assist that male in getting comfortable with expressing himself and easing himself into the actual office for face to face therapy.

**MEN -** This book is a reminder to express yourself and be free. This is also a tool to enhance your knowledge and awareness of all things "MAN." If you have difficulty verbally expressing yourself or have issues with finding ways to articulate what you want to say and/or how you feel, then write it or draw it out here. Set goals and affirmations and learn to plan and implement strategies in life.

**Parents -** Do you have a young boy that is on a path to finding himself in this life journey for "MANhood"? Try this as a tool to assist in navigating the tough topics. Imagine given your teen this book/journal and they complete it and refer to it a year or two years later to see how much they have grown or remained the same? This is also a way of knowing what one should work on good or bad.

**Partners -** What if there was a way for you to know what your MAN was thinking? Have you been in a situation and was unable to know or understand why he displayed certain actions, responded with certain reactions, or just wanted to really know what he has on his mind? What if you provided this book to him, he completes it, and gives it back to you? At this point, you will then know how to approach certain situations or gain an understanding of what his potential triggers are, what makes him sad, why he has difficulty opening up, and so much more.

**And all in between...**